AF488407

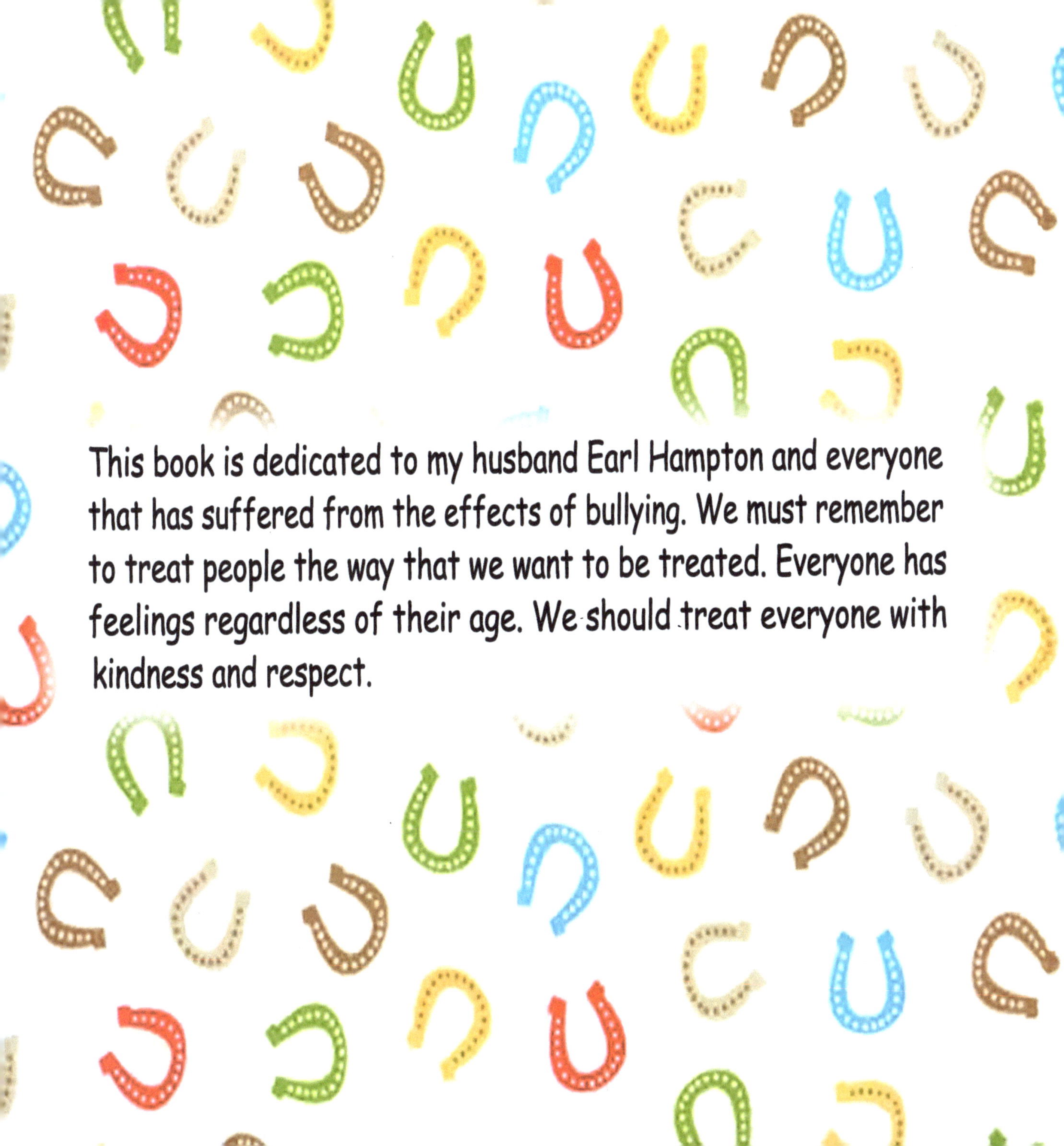

This book is dedicated to my husband Earl Hampton and everyone that has suffered from the effects of bullying. We must remember to treat people the way that we want to be treated. Everyone has feelings regardless of their age. We should treat everyone with kindness and respect.

Introduction

Today was a typical day at Hampton Farms in New Marketville. All the horses, including Sassy and Bro Man, were grazing in the pasture. The chicken was crowing, serving as the alarm clock to all the other animals. The rabbits were snuggled inside of their pen, wiggling and twitching their tiny noses. The peacocks were sitting high on their tree branches, making the usual screeching sound which is their way of saying hello. The goats went with their usual tradition of bleating and expressing their needs. Last, but not least, the turkeys were communicating by gobbling in the only way they knew how. Each animal was different in personality, feature, color, size, and age, but the one thing that they had in common was that they all lived on the farm together.

As Sassy joyfully walked across the pasture with her short legs dressed in her salmon pink tutu, she hung her head low as if almost touching the ground. Her painted splashes of white and light brown spots complimented her miniature-sized body. She wore a beautiful salmon pink and apple green ribbon tied in her long tan mane that was blowing gracefully in the wind. Sassy was headed to a birthday party at Hampton Farms.

Bro Man, the only regular-sized painted horse, was also excited. He had been chosen to help with the birthday party. He put on his best western jacket and polished his hoofs, for he wanted to impress all the little children too.

DAY

The animals at Hampton Farms watched attentively while Bro Man and Sassy prepared for the big event. They whispered and laughed to each other loud enough for Sassy to hear everything that was being said. They joked about Sassy's small frame and spotted body. They also made fun of Bro Man because of his dark brown and white spots.

Once Sassy realized the other animals were laughing and calling them names, she became sad. Bro Man told Sassy to just ignore the other animals. He stated, "If they do not want to play with you, then they are missing out on a good friend." They should always be open-minded to meeting new friends and should not judge anyone because of their size or color. They do not realize you could make a difference in their lives. You must learn from their mistreatment to never look down on anyone and be a bully. Take the negative energy and learn from it and treat people how you want to be treated." Sassy did not respond, but stood quietly, still holding her head down.

HAPPY BIRTHDAY
FROM
HAMPTON FARMS
SASSY

Now the party was about to begin. Sassy wanted to cheerfully greet the guest of honor, Aim, but she felt so disheartened that she just could not put a simple smile on her face. As she approached Aim, she was trying so hard to hold back her tears, but her big brown eyes were filling up fast. A tear hit the ground that seemed large enough for a goldfish to swim in. Sassy could not understand why the other animals were so mean to her and called her names She always tried to be nice to every animal at Hampton Farms. She would even share her food with them.

As Aim and Ason brushed Sassy's mane, they whispered to her, "It's going to be okay. It does not matter if you are small, large, thin, or heavy, you are beautiful and smart. We are now your new friends."

HAPPY
H DAY

Bro Man noticed the other animals were still laughing from across the pasture. He galloped over to Sassy because he observed that she was growing even quieter. He did not realize their rude demeanor bothered her to where she could no longer enjoy the party. As he approached her, she told him that the other animals were still calling her names because of her size and color. Bro Man responded, "They make fun of my color as well and I am only a little darker than you. I just smile at them because the jokes motivate me to be stronger and to work harder. Sometimes animals and people are mean and bully each other, but you must remember to treat them with kindness even if it is hard."

Aim and Ason clapped and complimented Bro Man by stating, "You are a good friend by saying such positive words to Sassy." The three of them together spoke words of encouragement to Sassy by adding, "You should allow this situation to motivate you to keep pressing forward. You are very talented and one of a kind. Let everyone, including those that bully, see that remaining positive can lead to self-motivation and high self-esteem."

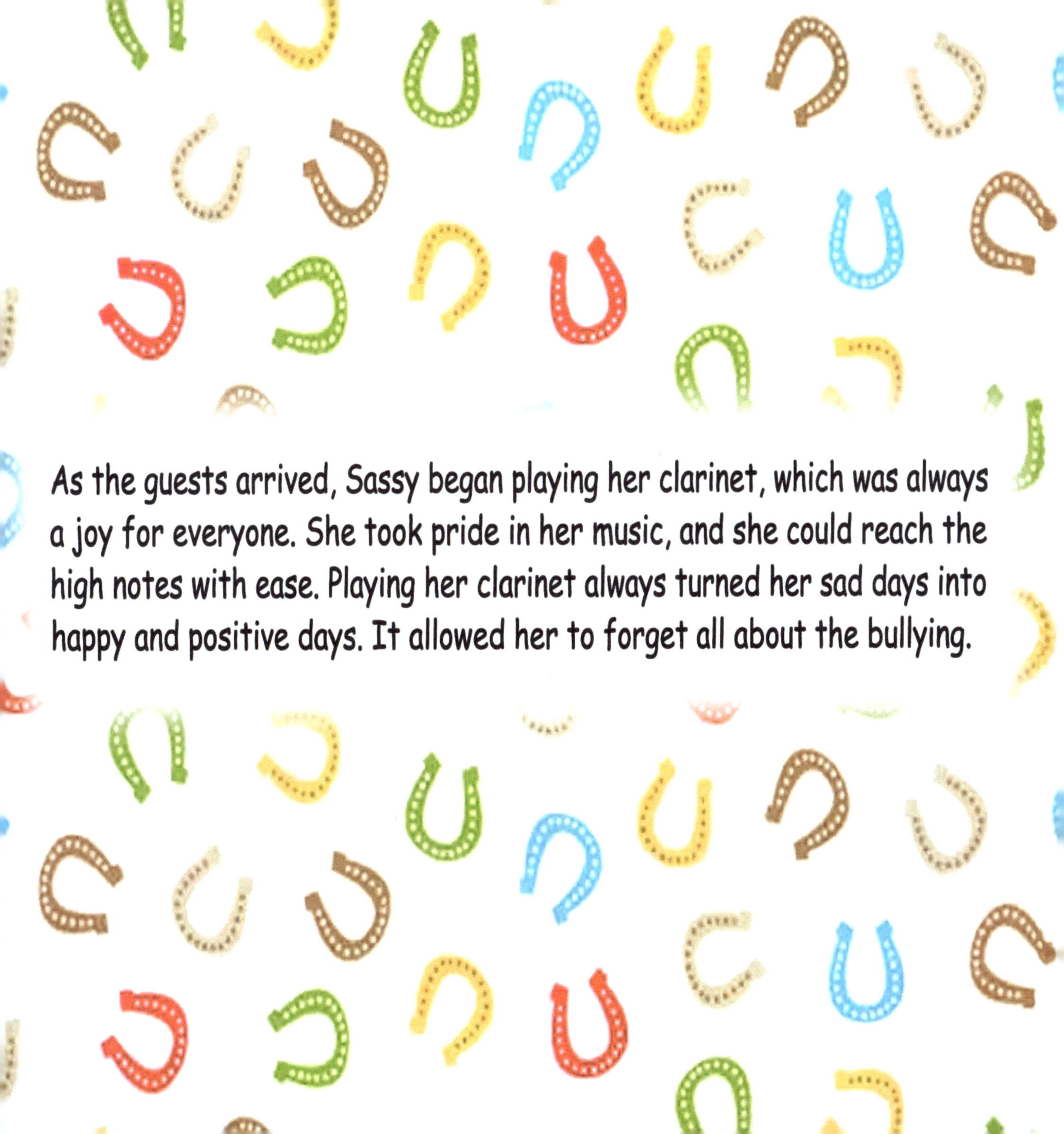

As the guests arrived, Sassy began playing her clarinet, which was always a joy for everyone. She took pride in her music, and she could reach the high notes with ease. Playing her clarinet always turned her sad days into happy and positive days. It allowed her to forget all about the bullying.

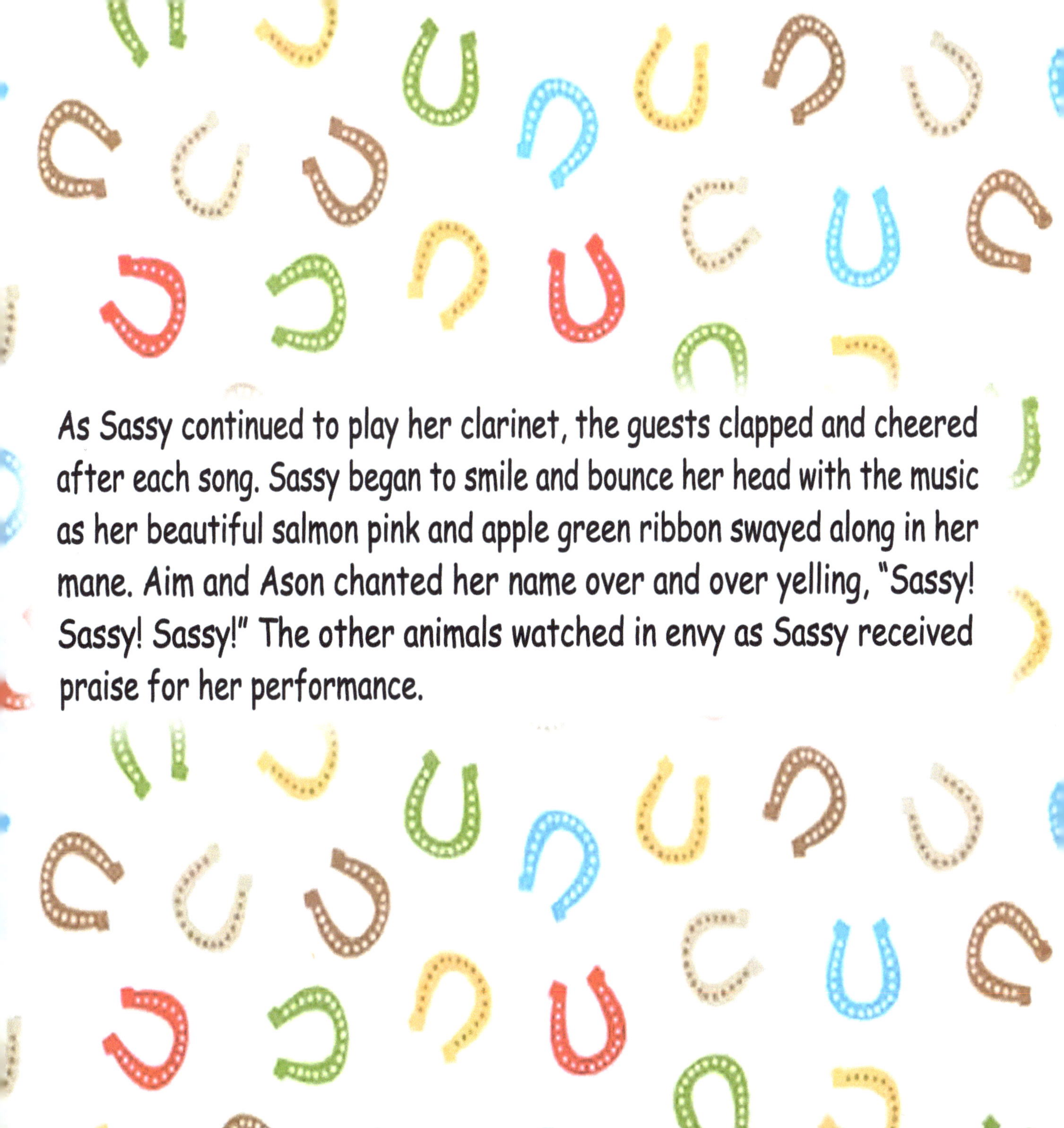

As Sassy continued to play her clarinet, the guests clapped and cheered after each song. Sassy began to smile and bounce her head with the music as her beautiful salmon pink and apple green ribbon swayed along in her mane. Aim and Ason chanted her name over and over yelling, "Sassy! Sassy! Sassy!" The other animals watched in envy as Sassy received praise for her performance.

HAMPTON
FARMS
HAMPTON
FARMS
HAMPTON
FARMS
NEW MARKET
HAPPY BIRTHDAY

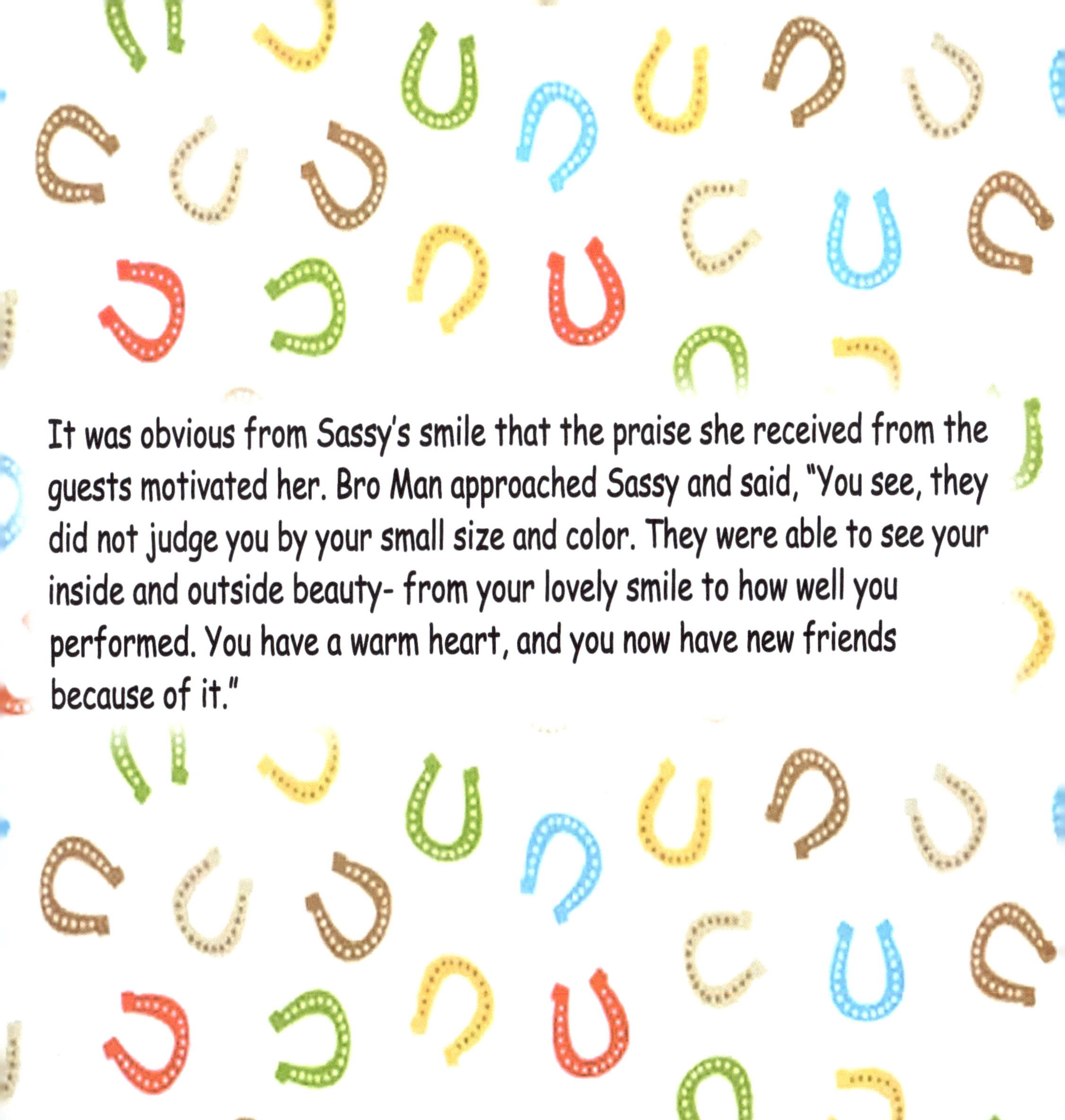

It was obvious from Sassy's smile that the praise she received from the guests motivated her. Bro Man approached Sassy and said, "You see, they did not judge you by your small size and color. They were able to see your inside and outside beauty- from your lovely smile to how well you performed. You have a warm heart, and you now have new friends because of it."

Sassy will always remember this event. Not only did she overcome a great deal of sadness, but she also met several friends. She had a feeling in her stomach she had never felt before. It was a feeling of happiness, joy, gratefulness, and blessing. At that moment, Sassy knew no one could ever make her feel bad again. She was no longer ashamed of her miniature size and spotted colors. She was very proud of everything that made her different from other animals.

NEW MARKETVILLE
HAMPTON FARMS

As the party ended, Sassy had a smile and glow that could be seen across the pasture. It was obvious that Bro Man, the guests, and her new friends, Aim and Ason, gave Sassy the support and motivation she needed. Sassy held her head high with pride as her beautiful long mane continued to blow in the wind. Her legs bounced higher as if she was floating in the sky. The other animals noticed her gleam and bounce. They looked at each other with their mouths open in disbelief. They were as quiet as little mice on cotton, for no one said anything negative.

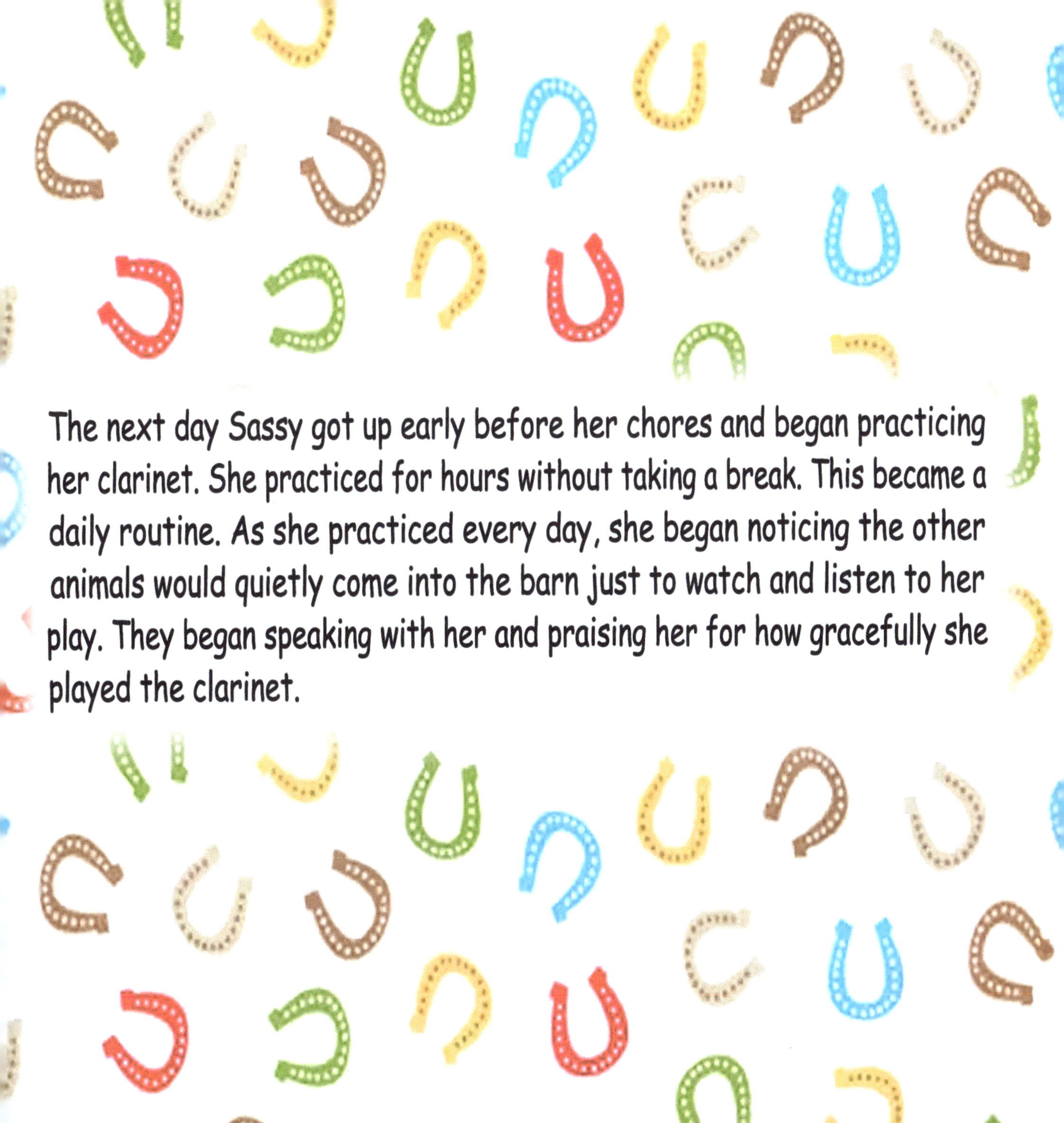

The next day Sassy got up early before her chores and began practicing her clarinet. She practiced for hours without taking a break. This became a daily routine. As she practiced every day, she began noticing the other animals would quietly come into the barn just to watch and listen to her play. They began speaking with her and praising her for how gracefully she played the clarinet.

JJ FARMS
MARKETTVILLE
SORRRRRYYY!!
GOBBLE, GOBBL
SORRRRRYYY

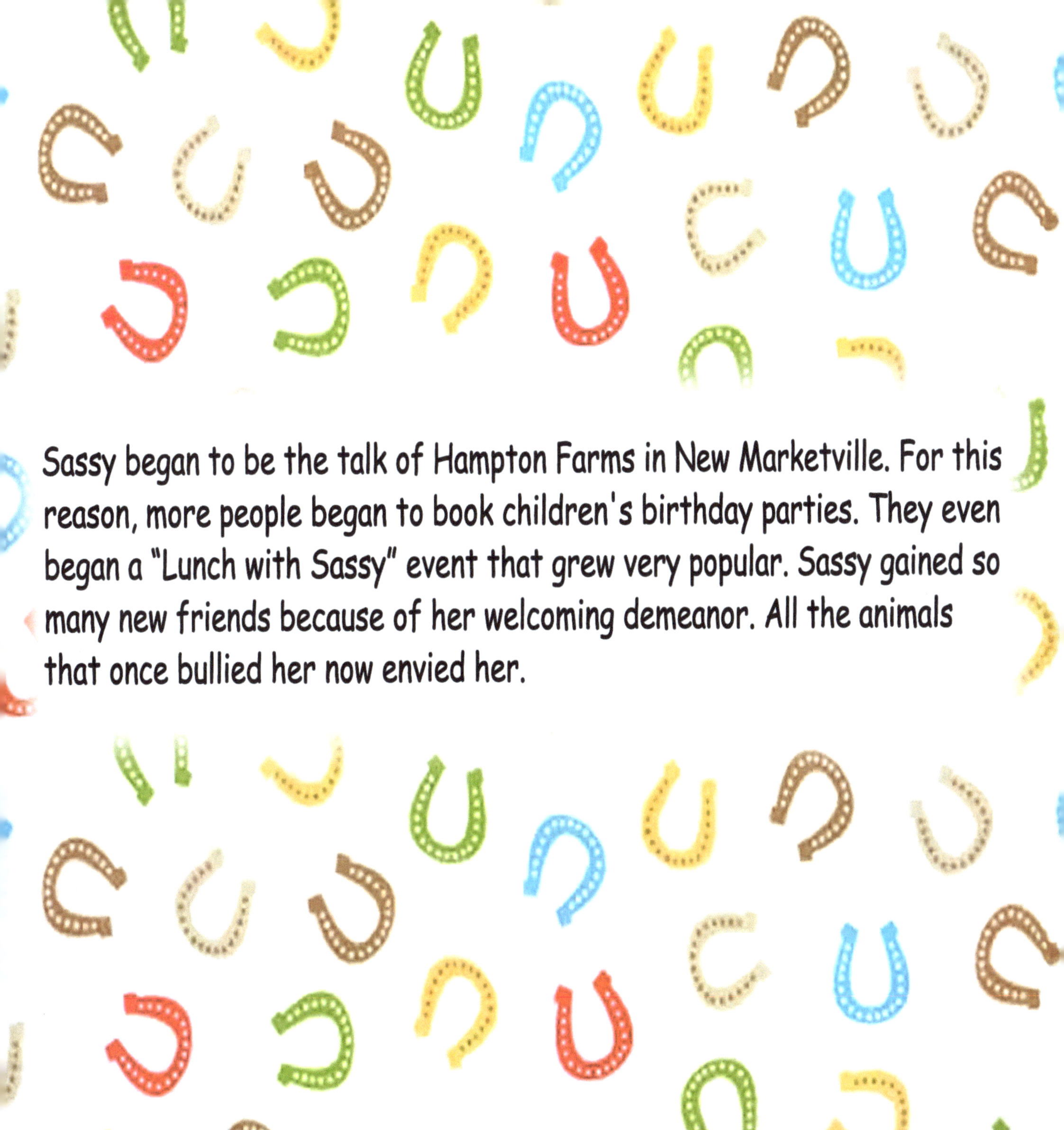

Sassy began to be the talk of Hampton Farms in New Marketville. For this reason, more people began to book children's birthday parties. They even began a "Lunch with Sassy" event that grew very popular. Sassy gained so many new friends because of her welcoming demeanor. All the animals that once bullied her now envied her.

FARMS
FARM
H FARMS ...
MEET & GREET

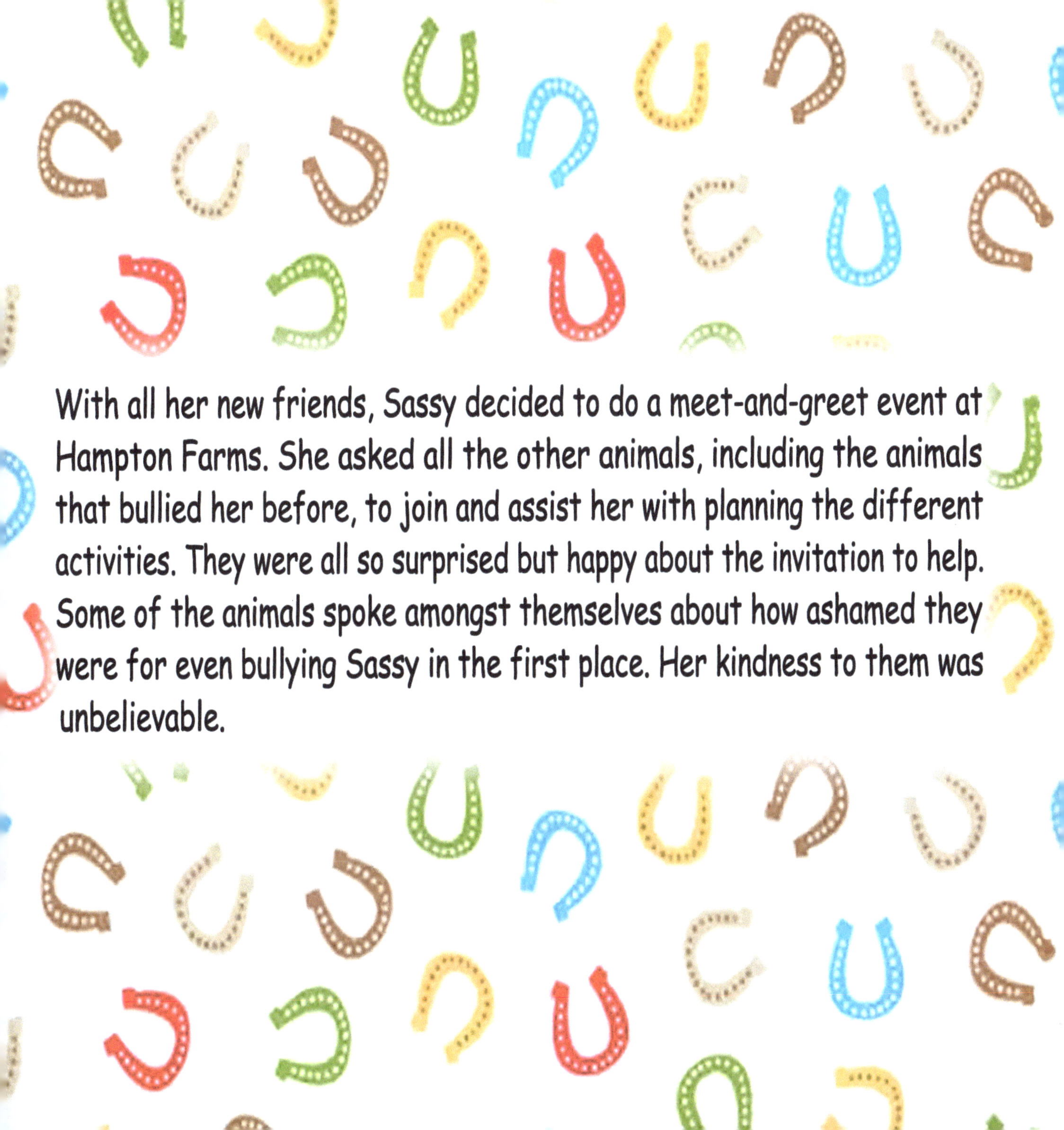

With all her new friends, Sassy decided to do a meet-and-greet event at Hampton Farms. She asked all the other animals, including the animals that bullied her before, to join and assist her with planning the different activities. They were all so surprised but happy about the invitation to help. Some of the animals spoke amongst themselves about how ashamed they were for even bullying Sassy in the first place. Her kindness to them was unbelievable.

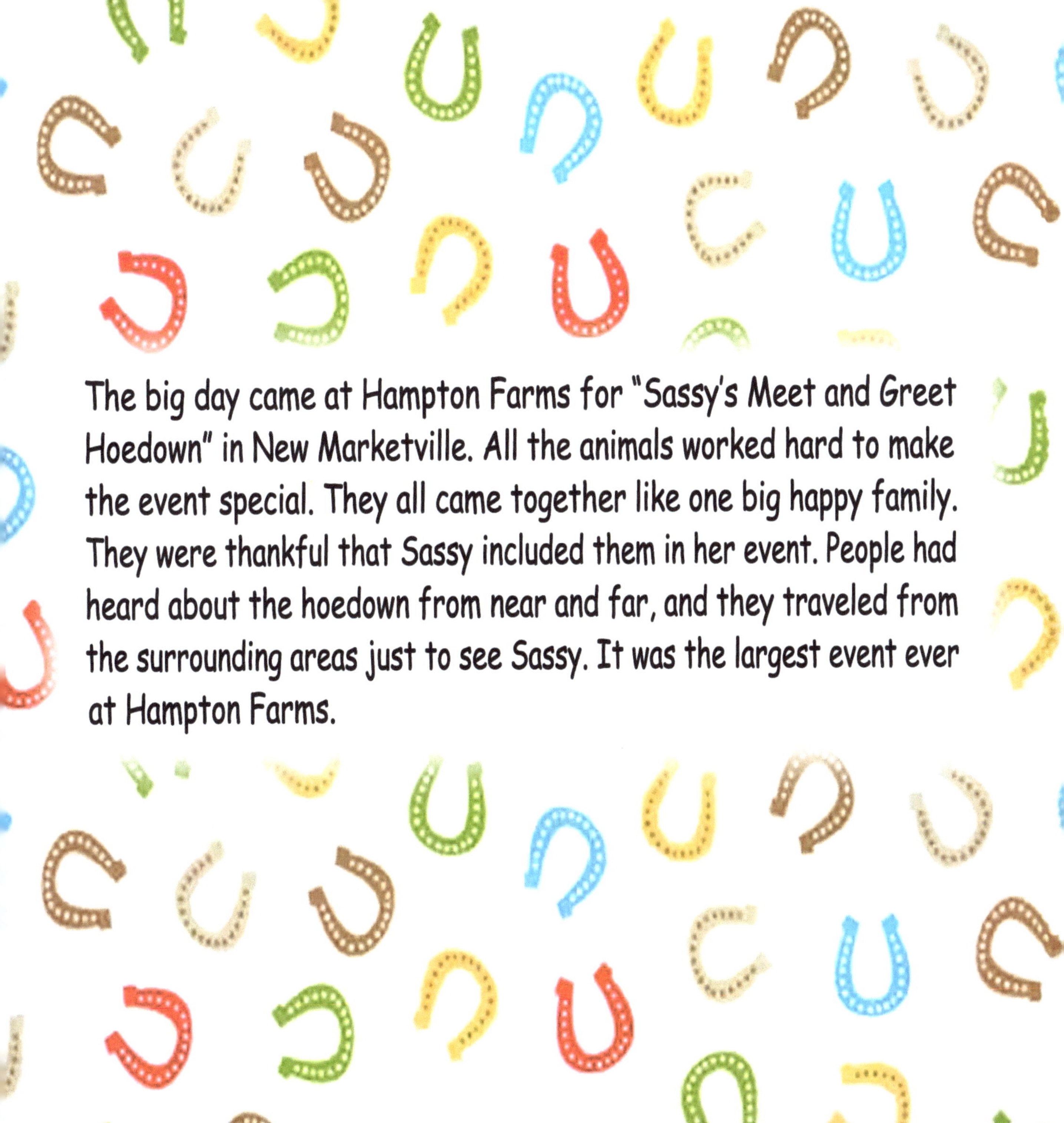

The big day came at Hampton Farms for "Sassy's Meet and Greet Hoedown" in New Marketville. All the animals worked hard to make the event special. They all came together like one big happy family. They were thankful that Sassy included them in her event. People had heard about the hoedown from near and far, and they traveled from the surrounding areas just to see Sassy. It was the largest event ever at Hampton Farms.

HAMPTO
FARMS

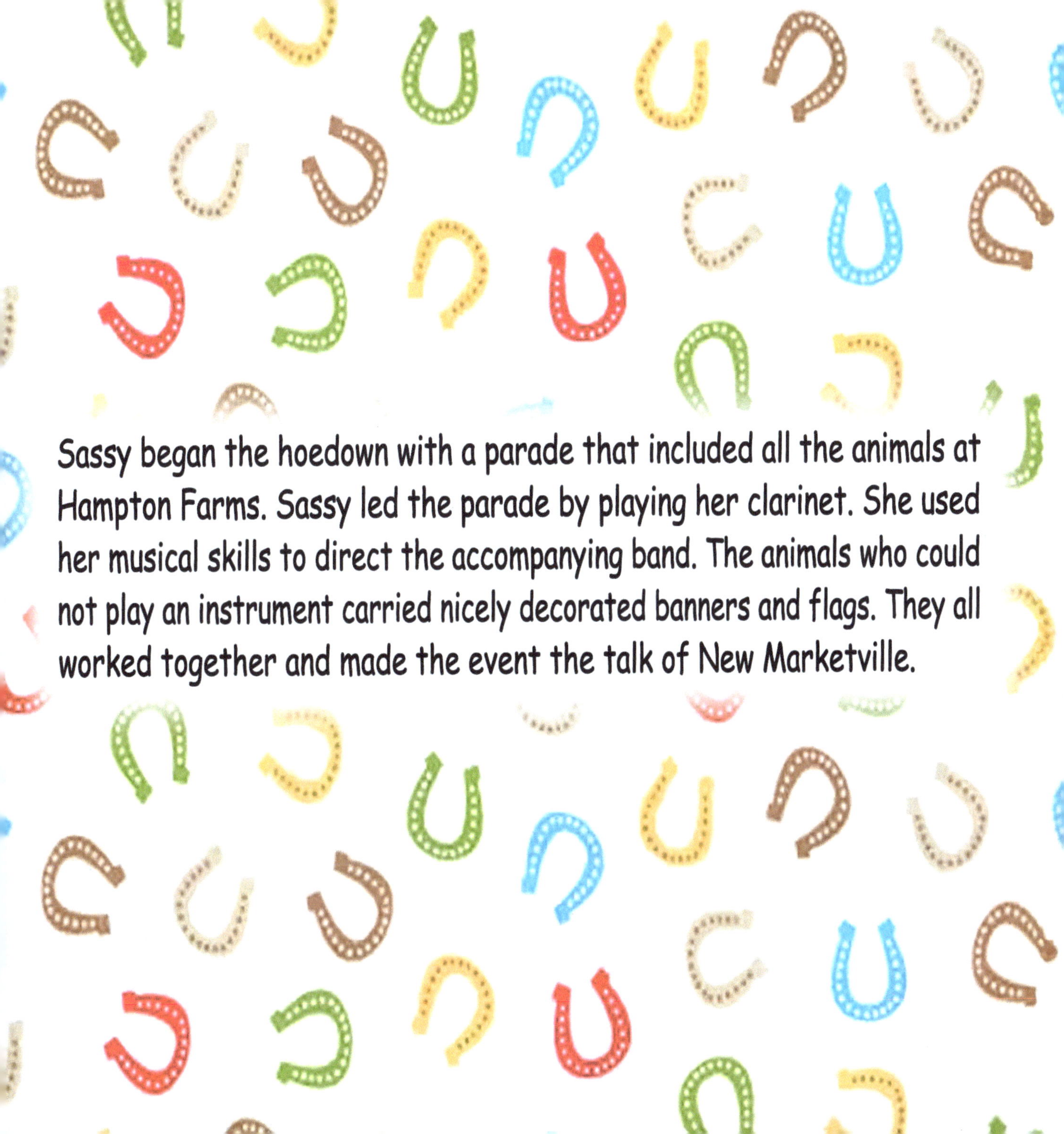

Sassy began the hoedown with a parade that included all the animals at Hampton Farms. Sassy led the parade by playing her clarinet. She used her musical skills to direct the accompanying band. The animals who could not play an instrument carried nicely decorated banners and flags. They all worked together and made the event the talk of New Marketville.

NO
BULLYING
ZONE

Sassy's Hoedown became a yearly event at Hampton Farms. Although Sassy faced years of bullying, she never mentioned to the other animals how their mistreatment made her feel .She always strived to treat them as her equals. The animals did realize this, so they apologized to Sassy one by one. In response to their apology, she smiled and gave each of them a great big hug. The animals made it their motto to always treat each other with kindness and respect and to never judge anyone for their color, height, or weight.

Epilogue:

Sassy continued to play her clarinet and be a good friend to all the animals at Hampton Farms. The animals hung up signs in the barn and all around the farm in big letters that stated, "NO BULLYING." They made it known to each other and to the newly arriving animals that Hampton Farms was a no-bullying zone.

It does not matter if you are an animal or human, we all have feelings. We all have different features and personalities. We are all one of a kind. You never know how anyone may be feeling inside. We should be nice and treat everyone with respect. If you see someone feeling down, say kind and uplifting words to make him or her feel better. Sometimes a simple smile will suffice. A kind word or gesture can make someone feel better. Bullying can be very hurtful and can make a person sad. Remember to treat everyone the way that you want to be treated.